Your Body:

2. Blood and Lungs

Dr. Gwynne Vevers

Illustrated by Sarah Pooley

LOTHROP, LEE & SHEPARD BOOKS
New York

OTHER TITLES IN THIS SERIES
Skin and Bone
Feeding and Digestion
Muscles and Movement

Text copyright © 1983 by Gwynne Vevers
Illustrations © 1983 by Sarah Pooley
First published in Great Britain in 1983 by The Bodley Head
All rights reserved. No part of this book may be reproduced or utilized in any form or by
any means, electronic or mechanical, including photocopying, recording or by any
information storage and retrieval system, without permission in writing from the
Publisher. Inquiries should be addressed to Lothrop, Lee & Shepard Books, a division
of William Morrow & Company, Inc., 105 Madison Avenue, New York, New York 10016.
Printed in the United States of America.
First U.S. Edition   1 2 3 4 5 6 7 8 9 10
Library of Congress Cataloging in Publication Data
Vevers, Gwynne, 1916-
  Your body.
  Includes index.
  Contents: 1. Skin and Bone—2. Blood and lungs— [etc.]—4. Muscles and movement.
  1. Body, Human—Juvenile literature. 2. Body, Human. I. Pooley, Sarah, ill. II. Title.
QP37.V48   1983   612   83-18757
ISBN 0-688-02823-3
ISBN 0-688-02824-1 (lib. bdg.)

Blood

You need a source of energy in order to keep your body active and to maintain a constant body temperature of 98.6°F (37°C). This source of energy is provided by food, but water and oxygen are also essential to your body.

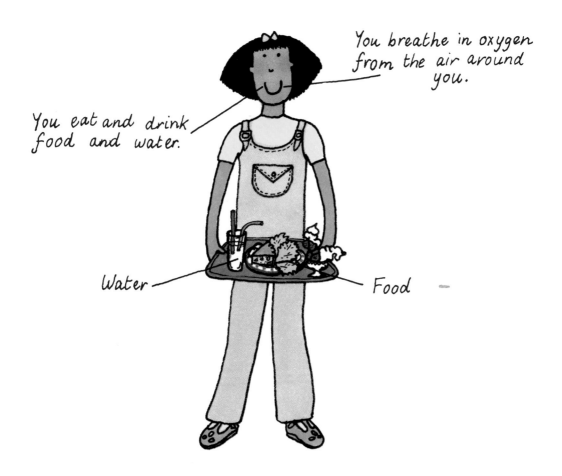

You breathe in oxygen from the air around you.

You eat and drink food and water.

Water

Food

The food and water that you eat and drink pass down into your stomach for digestion. When food is digested in the stomach it becomes semiliquid. It is absorbed into the blood and carried to the liver, which regulates the supply of nourishment to all parts of the body.

Oxygen is taken into your lungs from the air that surrounds you, and this happens particularly when you are running or jumping. The deeper you breathe, the more oxygen reaches the lungs.

To turn the food and oxygen into energy, your body needs a transport system to carry these substances to all parts of the body. This is done by the blood.

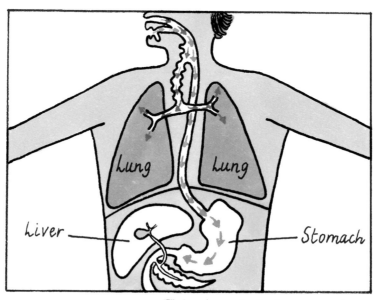

FOLLOW THE BLUE ARROWS ➡ This is what happens to the food and water you eat and drink.

FOLLOW THE RED ARROWS ➡ This is what happens to the air you breathe in through your nose.

THE HEART

My heart is actually the same size as my clenched fist, and its position is shown in this chest X ray.

The heart

Blood does not move around your body by itself. It has to be pumped around by your heart, a very special organ about the size of your clenched fist. Its walls are made of a special kind of muscle, heart muscle. Unlike the muscles in your arms, legs, or other parts of your body, the heart muscle never becomes tired and is always working, even when you are asleep.

Your heart goes on working even when you are asleep.

SNORE!

SNORE!

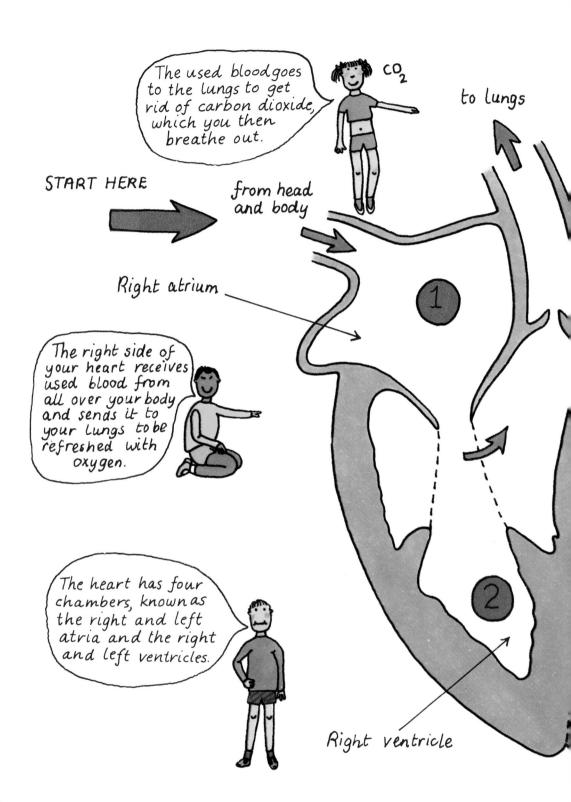

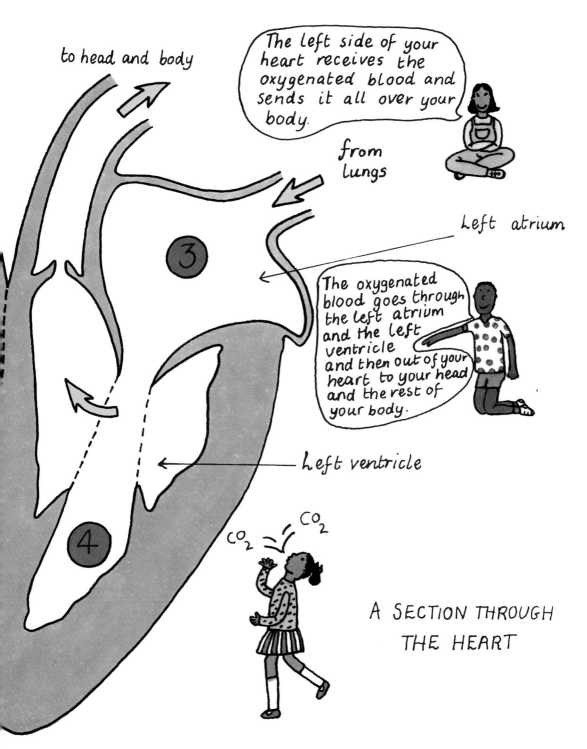

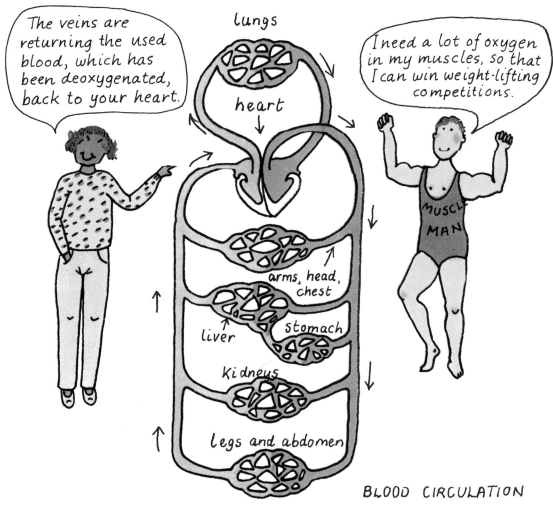

BLOOD CIRCULATION

Blue = deoxygenated blood
Pink = oxygenated blood

Blood travels around your body in muscular tubes known as arteries and veins. The arteries, which carry blood rich in oxygen and food materials, divide into tiny thin-walled blood vessels, called capillaries.

Oxygen is able to pass through the capillary walls into the cells of the body tissues, such as the muscles in your arms and legs. At the same time the capillaries bring liquid nourishment to these cells.

The blood leaving the capillaries has lost some of its oxygen and has also picked up waste matter produced by the body's tissues. The capillaries then join together to form the veins, which return blood to the heart, and so the whole cycle starts again.

The arteries carry blood from your heart.

The spidery blood vessels are called capillaries.

The heart pumps the blood through the blood vessels by contracting at regular intervals. Each contraction of the heart gives a heartbeat. Your doctor listens to the beats of your heart with a stethoscope. You can do the same by putting your ear to one end of a cardboard tube and the other end on your friend's chest.

In a healthy person the heart beats about 70 times a minute, and this goes on throughout life. This means that your heart beats about 40 million times a year. If you are excited or running a race, your heartbeats may increase to 100 or more a minute. The heart of a baby beats even faster. This is because it needs more energy in relation to its size.

More than 5 quarts (about 5 liters) of blood are pumped by the heart in one minute.

When it is beating at a rate of 70 beats a minute, the heart pumps more than 5 quarts (about 5 liters) of blood every minute. You can tell how fast your heart is beating by feeling the pulse on the front of your wrist with your finger. Put your first two fingers on the thumb side of your wrist. As the heart contracts, a pressure wave passes along the artery that comes down your arm, like a ripple on the surface of water. You detect the ripple as it passes under your fingers.

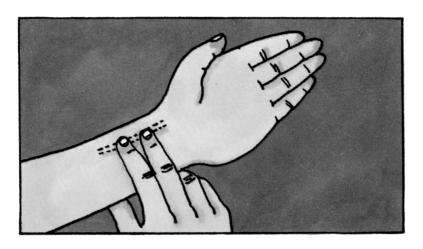

The blood circulation is very rapid. It takes 16 seconds for the blood to be pumped from your heart to your feet and back again, while the return journey from heart to brain, a much shorter distance, only takes about 6 seconds.

Slightly more than half the blood consists of a straw-colored liquid known as plasma. A little less than half is made up of tiny cells that can be seen only under a microscope. These are called red cells, white cells, and platelets.

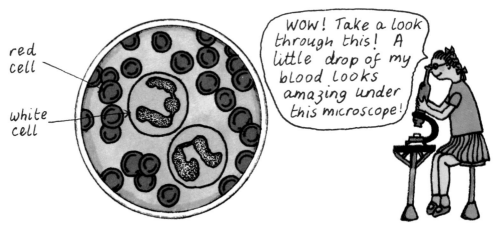

RED AND WHITE CELLS AS SEEN UNDER A MICROSCOPE

Red blood cells

Hemoglobin and I get along really well together.

The red cells are shaped like discs, with a dent on each side. They are being made all the time in the marrow of the bones, and each red cell lasts about 120 days. These cells are colored by a red pigment called hemoglobin that makes the blood appear red. Hemoglobin is very important because it can combine with a great deal of oxygen. In each drop of blood there are 5 million red blood cells.

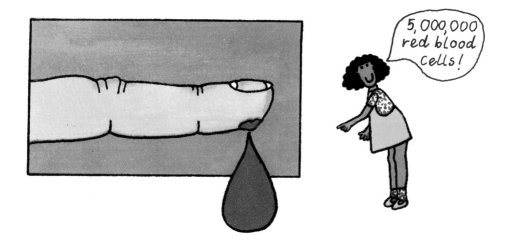

5,000,000 red blood cells!

A fat white cell after a good meal of bacteria.

The white blood cells do not have a fixed shape like the red cells. They change their shape as they move along the blood vessels, and there are only 7,000 to 10,000 of them in a drop of blood. The white cells move around in the bloodstream engulfing tiny particles, such as bacteria, that are harmful to the body because they may cause disease.

There are fewer white cells than red ones in a drop of blood—only about 7,000 to 10,000!

The much smaller platelets are important to us when we cut or scrape ourselves. The platelets help to produce a clot, which plugs the wound and seals it so that the blood cannot flow out. This clot, called a scab, is a brownish crust which also protects the wound against harmful bacteria that might get into the bloodstream. The white cells gather in great numbers near a wound and help to prevent infection.

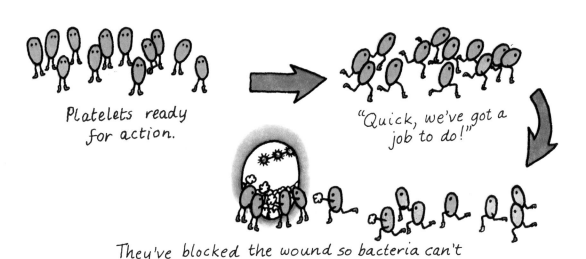

Platelets ready for action.

"Quick, we've got a job to do!"

They've blocked the wound so bacteria can't get through before the skin can heal.

Lungs

There are two lungs, the left lung and the right lung. When you breathe in, the air goes through your nose, where it is warmed and collects moisture, and then down your throat to your windpipe (trachea). Inside your nose there are tiny hairs that help to catch any dirt or dust that may be in the air. You can also breathe through your mouth when your nose is blocked by, for instance, a cold. Your nose produces a liquid called mucus. When you blow your nose, you blow out mucus, and with it, dust and germs.

Behind the upper part of the breastbone, the trachea divides into two main tubes, the left bronchus which leads the air into the left lung, and the right bronchus which leads the air into the right lung.

In the lung each bronchus divides up again and again into a large number of thinner tubes, called the respiratory bronchioles, which resemble the branches of a tree.

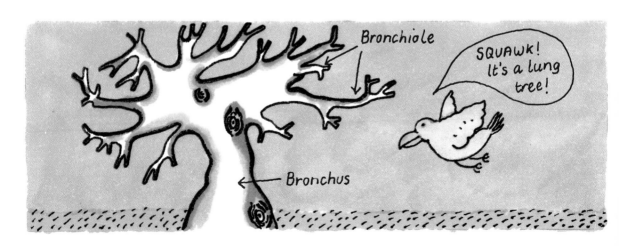

Each bronchiole ends in many tiny air sacs. There are about 350 million air sacs in each lung, and if all these were laid out flat on the ground, they would cover the surface of a tennis court.

Each air sac in the lungs is surrounded by a
network of very tiny capillaries. This is where the
blood in the capillaries meets the air with its oxygen.

The capillaries cover the surface of each air sac very closely, so that the oxygen in the air can pass through the capillary walls into the blood, where it is taken up by the hemoglobin pigment in the red cells. At the same time the waste substance carbon dioxide, which is also dissolved in the blood, passes out through the capillary walls into the air sacs and leaves the body when you breathe out. In yawning, when you are sleepy, bored, or needing fresh air, you take in a long, slow breath and let it out slowly.

This is your rib cage, enclosing your two lungs and heart.

At the bottom is the diaphragm, which flattens when you breathe in! Look!

Your heart and lungs lie in a cage made up of your ribs at the sides, and at the bottom a dome-shaped sheet of muscle known as the diaphragm (the "g" is not pronounced). When you breathe in, the muscles of your chest pull the ribs outward and slightly upward, and at the same time the diaphragm becomes flatter. This expands the chest so that air is drawn into the lungs. When you breathe out, the chest muscles relax. The used air is pushed out of the lungs, through the trachea, and out of the nose and mouth. This goes on all the time, even when you are asleep.

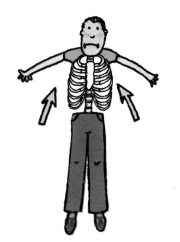

BREATHING IN

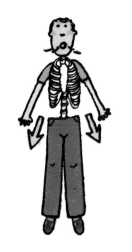

BREATHING OUT

Try this simple exercise. Take in a very big breath through your mouth and watch your chest get bigger. Then, after a few seconds, close your mouth and try to blow out your stomach.

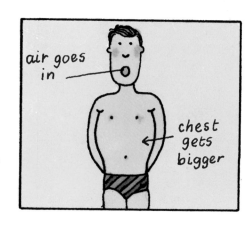

air goes in

chest gets bigger

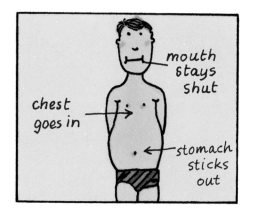

mouth stays shut

chest goes in

stomach sticks out

As you do so, your chest goes in. You will have pushed the air down into the bottom of the lungs and your diaphragm will have moved down toward your stomach, pushing it so that it sticks out.

Sometimes the bronchi are irritated by an infection or by a speck of dust. When this happens, you take in a deep breath and briefly close parts of the trachea so that air is held back in the lungs. Suddenly you let go, the trachea opens, and air is driven out of the lungs very rapidly to produce a cough.

COUGH! COUGH! COUGH! COUGH!

COUGH! COUGH! COUGH!

If smoking makes you cough, Dad, why do it?

SMOKING DAMAGES YOUR LUNGS! DON'T DO IT!!!

When your nose is irritated or "tickled" by dust or something else, air is pushed out of the lungs and through the nose to produce a sneeze. This helps to clear the dust from your nose. When you sneeze, the air is pushed out very fast, at a speed of almost 95 miles (about 150 km) per hour.

When you hiccup, air is taken into the lungs in rapid bursts. This happens when the diaphragm contracts very rapidly, with a kind of jerk. This may occur for a variety of reasons, such as long bursts of laughing or giggling.

Index

Page numbers in *italic type* indicate illustrations.